The
MEDITATION
Activist's
Travel
GUIDE

JILL KNELL

www.soulmaps.com.au

Cover design by Judith San Nicolas
Interior book design by Lorna Hendry
Typeset in Lora and Nunito Sans
Printed and bound in Australia by IngramSpark

Prepared for publication by Dr Juliette Lachemeier @
The Erudite Pen

A catalogue record for this
book is available from the
National Library of Australia

The Meditation Activist's Travel Guide – 1st edition
ISBN 978-0-6456028-0-7 Paperback
ISBN 978-0-6456028-1-4 Ebook

From inner space to
outer space, from I to We,
SOUL Meditations to take
around the world.

*We're all just walking
each other home.*

Ram Dass

Dedication

I dedicate this travel guide to my
wonderfully co-generative Soul Maps
community. You have given generously
and gracefully of your beautiful energy.
I love and honour you all.

And to my beloveds.
I am because you are.

Jill Knell
August 2022

*When you do things from
the Soul, you feel a river
moving in you, a joy.*

Rumi

Contents

Introduction

*Whatever is happening,
this is the path to
enlightenment.*

Pema Chodron

These are interesting times. Our internal worlds are increasingly touched by local and global events and experiences that disturb our inner peace. The pathways to hope and optimism as well as to worry and despair are laid out for us. We get to choose which path to take.

Of course, our logical mind wants to choose what we perceive as the 'positive' path. However, despite our best intentions, sometimes we can be beset by a sense of hopelessness as to how we can best contribute to a better life for ourselves and others, and to a better world.

In this travel guide I would like to offer you some contemplative pathways of love, truth, peace and integrity.

For me, and many others, meditation is a powerful tool to nurture our inner worlds. It also gives us an incredible opportunity to consciously send our best intentions out into the waking world where they are soul-ly needed. Meditation helps us to be and do our very best.

When I first heard the term 'Meditation Activist' I knew it captured the essence of how I've been trying to show up and contribute to the meditation communities I am part of.

Meditation activism is about putting our inner selves out there (together and alone) to transform society. It supports us to transcend our three main tasks in life: to wake up, to grow up and to show up. If we're going to rise, we may as well shine.

This is practical spirituality in action – soulfully combining our head, heart, hands and spirit in all we do.

Overview

*You may follow one stream.
Realise that it leads to the
Ocean, but do not mistake
the stream for the Ocean.*

Jan-Fishan Khan

The experience of meditating is one of
transcendence. It calms and focuses
the mind to allow our inner wonderfulness
to emerge. There are many different
meditation teachers and practices.

The Meditation Activist's Travel Guide
provides a unique way to enhance soulful
practices that nurture our inner and
outer worlds.

In this travel guide, 'soul' (or being whole),
is defined as the vibrant integration of these
four domains:

- Head: truth, envisaging, intellectual intelligence, totally inspired.
- Heart: love, embracing, emotional intelligence, heart wide open.
- Hands: integrity, embodying, worldly intelligence, fully alive.
- Spirit: peace, evolving, spiritual intelligence, absolutely present.

This travel guide outlines the purpose of a SOUL meditation, provides a suggested meditation pathway and offers nine different soulful meditations.

To chaperon you into and out of your meditation, you may already have some techniques that you use. You are invited to experience the SOUL Meditations Four-Step Pathway as a portal into liminal space and for re-entry into the world.

The meditations are simple and contemplative with a combination of inner inquiry, guided visualisation, focussed intent and, this is the activist's part, consciously sharing your inner wisdom with the planet and all sentient beings.

Each meditation has been designed around a specific focus to share with the world. The aim is to support you to move deeply into a space of calm connection with your inner wisdom and to radiate that wisdom out into the world where it's most needed.

You can decide which meditation you are drawn to. They can be used in any order but are listed alphabetically.

A brief meaning of the title of each meditation is included. There are a number of inspirational quotes for each meditation that will hopefully inspire and delight you.

Each meditation has three reflective intentions that you can choose from to take with you on your travels.

There is also a SOUL Songs Souvenir Playlist with nine soulful songs for each meditation that you may like to enjoy either before or after you come back from your travels. Singing with or even just listening to the SOUL Songs is a beautiful way to continue to share your inner wisdom with the world. There is a QR code for each playlist at the end of each chapter.

If you'd like to listen to a voice-guided version of each meditation, please scan the QR code below to take you to the 'SOUL Meditations to take around the world' podcast on Spotify.

Nine custom-designed embodied moving meditation yoga sequences have been developed by Melisah Feeney (the Flowing Yogini) to align with each playlist. You can scan the QR code below to access the YouTube channel 'Yoga with Soul'.

Podcast
SOUL Meditations to take around the world on Spotify

Yoga
Yoga with Soul: embodied moving meditations with Melisah Feeney on YouTube

Purpose of a SOUL Meditation

The purpose of a SOUL Meditation is to calm ourselves, connect with our inner wisdom and consciously send that wisdom out in the world where it's most needed. A simple way of remembering the purpose of a SOUL Meditation is:

S is for Seed the Space

Give yourself permission to stop thinking what you're thinking or doing what you're doing or feeling what you're feeling. Consciously create a sacred circuit-breaking space. Settle your body, your mind and your breath so you can prepare to share the wisdom of your inner journey with the outer world.

O is for Observe and Open

Observe what's going on inside yourself, what thoughts, feelings and sensations are present. Open yourself to stillness – calm, unruffled conscious awareness. Open yourself to the whole of which we're all part.

U is for Understand and Utilise

Understand you are not your body, your thoughts or your feelings. You are timeless self always connected to your inner wisdom. You can utilise your inner wisdom to transform your conscious awareness and send it out into the waking world to enrich your life and the lives of all sentient beings.

L is for Live Life

Know that your inner wisdom is ever present in your waking life, and you can live from a place of soul connection with every conscious breath. Know that worldly distractions will come and go but, at your centre, you are part of divine consciousness.

SOUL
Meditation
Four-Step
Pathway

Outline

Seed the Space

Create space

Select meditation, enjoy inspirations
and choose reflective intention

Prepare body and breath (9*)

Go on Soul Stroll

Relax and enjoy

Open and Observe

Focus on chosen reflective intention

Open to inner wisdom messages

Observe and trust your intuition

Understand and Utilise

Choose inner wisdom message
to share with world

Chose how to share message

Travel out to the world

Hold the space of oneness

Live Life

Return from your travels
back into heart centre

Move into waking world

Capture insights

Explore SOUL Songs Souvenir Playlists

Listen to guided SOUL Meditations
to take around the world

Experiment with Yoga with SOUL

Seed the Space

Make space. Temporally and physically. Schedule some 'you' time by making a date with yourself. Around twenty minutes should do. Move into a place that is quiet and will be uninterrupted for the duration of your travels.

Choose one of the SOUL Meditations in this travel guide. Let yourself be drawn to the SOUL meaning that most resonates with you.

Enjoy refreshing yourself with the inspirations specific to your chosen meditation.

Decide which of the reflective intentions, outlined in your chosen meditation, that you'd like to bring into the liminal space with you. You can bring more than one if you'd like.

Start by preparing your body and breath.

Sit or lie with your spine as straight as is comfortable.

Close your eyes.

Pay attention to your breath by taking three deep breaths or use the Nine-Star (9*) Breath technique. 9* breathing is three rounds of breathing in for three seconds, holding the breath for three seconds and breathing out for three seconds.

Then just let the breath breathe itself.

Open and Observe

Now it's time to go on a Soul Stroll. Enter into liminal space by imagining yourself in a beautiful natural environment. This can be any scenario of your choosing. It might be a forest, a garden, a mountain, a river, a beach or an ocean. Somewhere you feel comfortable, calm, connected and collected. Immersed in nature.

Bring the scene clearly into your mind's eye. Colour it in and make it shine. Use all your senses to ground you in this environment: smell, sound, sight, taste, sensation, temperature, texture.

You may choose to stay still, move through or interact with your environment.

Relax and enjoy.

When you're ready, gently bring one or more of your chosen reflective intentions into your mind and observe what happens.

Be aware of what may arise, what you might notice in or around you. Notice any inner wisdom messages that might come to you. They could manifest in the form of images, thoughts, feelings, sounds or sensations. They may be intense or subtle.

Trust your intuition.

Feel your head, heart, hands and spirit expand and resonate with any inner wisdom messages. Feel the power of your inner wisdom messages moving through you.

STEP 3

Understand and Utilise

Consciously choose one inner wisdom message that you would like to share with the world. It could be in the form of words, images, thoughts, feelings, sounds or colour.

Maybe it's like the light of a candle flame that glows out and ignites the flame in others without diminishing itself.

Maybe it's like the whisper of the wind that gently blows across the planet cleansing everything in its path.

Maybe it's like the surface of water that flows out bringing an end to yearning.

Choose what is most powerful for you.

Picture your heart centre resonating with the form of your inner wisdom message. Let it spread throughout your whole body. Feel its truth, strength and power. Then intensify it further and feel it expanding and moving outside you and travelling out into your immediate environment. There is a sense of irresistibility as it moves further and further out to embrace and transform the waking world.

Resonating, expanding, embracing, transforming.

There may be specific people, other sentient beings and certain places that you want to travel to and direct your inner wisdom message more intensively towards.

Imagine yourself connected to the whole planet and all living beings. One heart, one breath, one song, one world.

Stay with the power of the whole for a while.

Live Life

When you are ready, feel the inner wisdom message moving back from the world into your immediate environment and then back into your heart centre.

The fragrance of your message will linger across the world as well as in your heart centre, where it will remain and be accessible at any time.

Trust that you already know what else (if anything) you might need to know or do as you return from your travels.

Then just allow yourself to move gently back into the waking world feeling calm, connected and collected.

You might like to capture your insights with words, images or sounds.

There are nine SOUL Songs Souvenir Playlists, one for each meditation. Each playlist has nine soulful songs. You may like to enjoy some SOUL Songs after you come back from your travels.

Singing with or even just listening to the SOUL Songs is a beautiful way to continue to share your inner wisdom with the world.

If you'd prefer to close your eyes and be led on another journey, the Spotify podcast 'SOUL Meditations to take around the world' features nine voice-guided episodes, one for each meditation.

There are nine custom-designed yoga sequences on YouTube titled 'Yoga with Soul embodied moving meditations.'

The 9 SOUL
Meditations

SOULace Meditation: Exactly As It Is

SOULace is coming to terms with what is, finding comfort and consolation in the most difficult of times. It's about holding the space for those in distress or suffering. It's about heartfelt compassion and trying not to take things personally. It's honouring our emergent destiny.

(from solace: to comfort, to console, soothe or offer relief from suffering)

SOULace reflective intentions

Accept that this too
shall pass.

Hope that all beings will
be free from suffering.

Let go, let come.

Inspirations

Happiness is like a tree going into the sky, and sadness is like the roots going down to the womb of the earth. Both are needed. The bigger the tree, the bigger will be its roots. In fact, it is always in proportion. That's its balance. OSHO

Whether this moment is happy or not depends on you. It's you who makes the moment happy, not the moment that makes you happy. With mindfulness, concentration and, insight, any moment can become a happy moment.
THICH NHAT HANH

When the resistance is gone, so are the demons.
PEMA CHODRON

The wise are not tossed with the ups and downs of the wave of happiness and misery. They dive deep into the spirit-ocean of bliss, avoiding the storms of delusion.
PARAMAHANSA YOGANANDA

SOULace Songs Souvenir Playlist – Exactly As It Is

1. *Release* (Amrita Devi)
2. *Thank You* (Edo & Jo)
3. *Song of Life* (Bettina Maureen, Nick Barber)
4. *Hold My Hand* (Nessi Gomes)
5. *Time After Time* (Iron & Wine)
6. *Into Your Hands* (Deva Premal & Miten)
7. *You Can't Rush Your Healing* (Trevor Hall)
8. *Let Go* (Ixchel Prisma)
9. *You Are Safe* (Vanessa Forbes)

Playlist
SOULace Songs
on Spotify

SOULarium Meditation: Healing Light

SOULarium is about creating a space to connect with universal light and intensifying it with our own radiance in order to share with the planet. Conscious effulgence is radiating out healing love, peace, truth and integrity particularly to the darkest places.

(from solarium: a room using for bathing in therapeutic light)

SOULarium
reflective intentions

Share intense healing light
with the world.

Envelop every sentient being
with healing light.

See all sentient beings
connected in the light.

Inspiration

*Travel light, live light, spread
the light, be the light.*

YOGI BHAJAN

*I wish I could show you when you are
lonely or in the darkness, the astonishing
light of your own being.*

HAFIZ

It is your light that lights the world.

RUMI

*We have come into this exquisite
world to experience ever and ever
more deeply our divine courage,
freedom and light!*

HAFIZ

SOULarium Songs Souvenir Playlist – Healing Light

1. *I release control* (Alexa Sunshine Rose)
2. *In the Light of Love* (Deva Premal & Miten)
3. *I Am The Light Of My Soul* (Sirgun Kaur, Darshan Singh)
4. *Let The Light In* (Tara Divinia)
5. *The Long-time Sun* (Sirgun Kaur)
6. *I Am Light* (Citadel)
7. *Light of Love* (Jai-Jagdeesh)
8. *Divine Light Gayathri Mantra* (Tara Divina)
9. *Asatoma – From Darkness to Light* (Kevin James)

Playlist
SOULarium Songs
on Spotify

SOULdier Meditation: In Service of the Universe

To SOULdier is to stand up to
the ego and nurture courageous
strength for the inner battle
with the darkness in us all.
It's about self-discipline,
spiritual accountability and
inner empowerment. It's about
preparing ourselves for challenges
and putting in the effort to work
on ourselves so we can stand
in or move into the light.

(from soldier: a warrior, militant leader,
to push forward doggedly)

SOULdier
reflective intentions

Have inner strength to
fight the good fight.

Triumph over ego.

Be an evolutionary.

Inspirations

A man should be in constant rebellion
against himself, for the ego shrinks
and deforms like a concave mirror.
It is the worst of tyrants, for it totally
dominates you.

SRI NISARGADATTA MAHARAJ

Yesterday I was so clever I wanted to
change the world. Today I am wise
so I am changing myself.

RUMI

I would like my life to be as a statement
of love and compassion – and where it isn't,
that's where my work lies.

RAM DASS

Be patient. You'll know when it's time
for you to wake up and move ahead.

RAM DASS

SOULdier Songs
Souvenir Playlist – In Service of the Universe

1. *Please Prepare Me* (Beautiful Chorus)
2. *Wheel of Time* (Ayla Nereo)
3. *The Power is Here Now* (Alexia Chellun)
4. *Road to Freedom* (Deva Premal & Miten)
5. *We Shall Be Known* (MaMuse, Thrive Choir)
6. *Here In The Now* (Murray Kyle)
7. *More Than Love* (Trevor Hall)
8. *Life Uncommon* (Jewel)
9. *Wave of Women* (Heather Houston)

Playlist
SOULdier Songs
on Spotify

SOULidarity Meditation: In Divine Company

SOULidarity is deeply connecting with others through a shared value base, usually spiritual or ethical. It is consciously reaching out to others with powerful, positive intentions to co-create better lives and a better world, building intentional communities that nourish and nurture.

(from solidarity: unity based on common interests)

SOULidarity
reflective intentions

Nurture interconnectedness.

Transform fear into love.

Co-create conscious
community.

Inspirations

Let's trade in all our judging for
appreciating. Let's lay down our
righteousness and just be together.
RAM DASS

Be with those who help your being.
RUMI

There is a community of spirit.
Open your hands if you want to be held.
Move outside the tangle of fear-thinking.
Flow down and down in always
widening rings of being.
RUMI

We're fascinated by the words –
but where we meet is in the silence
behind them.
RAM DASS

SOULidarity Songs Souvenir Playlist – In Divine Company

1. *We Are Love* (Jai-Jagdeesh)
2. *We Bring Our Souls* (Freedom Family Band)
3. *Ancient Mother* (Lisa Dancing-Light)
4. *Calling All Angels* (MaMuse)
5. *Sweet Connections* (Murray Kyle)
6. *We Are All Related* (Nessi Gomes)
7. *My Own* (Trevor Hall)
8. *With You* (Jai-Jagdeesh)
9. *Reconnected* (Kyle Murray)

Playlist
SOULidarity Songs
on Spotify

SOULitude Meditation: Present at the Edge

SOULitude is about consciously moving away from outer distractions to connect with and nourish our inner world. To listen in silence to the quiet, calm inner voice or to be present with the stillness within. It supports us to connect with and affirm our strengths and values and to live from that place in love and not fear.

(from solitude: being alone, in a lonely place, secluded)

SOULitude
reflective intentions

Connect with inner stillness.

Create calm.

Honour the silence.

Inspirations

The answer lies within ourselves.
If we can't find peace and happiness there,
it's not going to come from the outside.
TENZIN PALOMA

When you look at that unchanging
Existence from the outside, you call it God;
and when you look at it from the inside
you call it yourself. It is but one.
SWAMI VIVEKANANDA

All that is required to realise the
Self is to be still.
BHAGAVAN SRI RAMANA MAHARISHI

Don't go outside your house to see flowers.
My friend, don't bother with that excursion.
Inside your body there are flowers.
One flower has a thousand petals.
That will do for a place to sit.
KABIR

SOULitude Songs Souvenir Playlist – Present at the Edge

1. *Inner Peace* (Beautiful Chorus)
2. *I Got Peace* (Chelsea Coy, DiElle)
3. *Blissful Stillness* (Kathy Zavada)
4. *Rooted* (Aisha Badru)
5. *Sacred* (Yaima)
6. *Waters* (Ajeet)
7. *Peace* (Ajeet)
8. *The Heart's Mystery* (Nick Barber)
9. *Soul Song* (Sacred Earth)

Playlist
SOULitude Songs
on Spotify

SOULutations Meditation: Rising in Love

SOULutations is greeting and meeting people as they are, where they are and honouring them for the inherent goodness that lies within us all. It's about not judging people. It's about rising above the individual and feeling the deeper interconnectedness between us all. It's a version of 'Namaste – I bow to you and the divine within you, that is also within me.'

(from salutations: an expression of greeting and goodwill)

SOULutations
reflective intentions

Honour the divine in
ourselves and others.

See the light in every heart.

Trust ourselves and
the Universe.

Inspirations

Finer than the finest, greater than
the greatest, that supreme self, soul
of the universe, is hidden in the hearts
of living creatures.
KATHA UPANISHAD

Make yourself so happy that when others
look at you, they become happy too.
YOGI BHAJAN

Be grateful for whoever comes.
Because each has been sent as a
guide from beyond.
RUMI

SOULutations Songs Souvenir Playlist – Rising in Love

1. *Shine* (Fia)
2. *Haseya* (Ajeet, Peia)
3. *Om Kama* (Deva Premal & Miten)
4. *Feel the Rhythm of your Heartbeat* (Mayana)
5. *So Much Magnificence* (Deva Premal & Miten)
6. *Trust* (Alexia Chellun)
7. *Shine* (Sacred Earth)
8. *Follow The Sun* (Xavier Rudd)
9. *Awakening* (Deva Premal, Miten)

Playlist
SOULutations Songs
on Spotify

SOULutions Meditation: The Great Knowing

SOULutions are answers that come from our inner knowing that serve the greater good. By allowing our heads to take a back-seat to our hearts and spirits we enable collective conscious awareness to arise. We see answers and ways forward that resonate in the service of evolution.

(from solution: an answer to a problem, moving beyond discontinuity, being fluid)

SOULutions
reflective intentions

Embrace not knowing.

Open to inner wisdom.

Live soulfully.

Inspirations

I have been a seeker, and I still am. But I stopped asking the books and the stars. I started listening to the teaching of my Soul.

RUMI

For things to reveal themselves to us, we need to be ready to abandon our views about them.

THICH NHAT HANH

You really do not need to know many things, but you definitely need to practice what you know.

SWAMI RAMA

SOULutions Songs Souvenir Playlist – The Great Knowing

1. *Breathe, Surrender* (Cup of Tea)
2. *The Art of Letting Go* (Fia)
3. *Calling* (Bliss)
4. *It's Easier* (Scarlet Crow)
5. *Guidance* (Shylah Ray Sunshine)
6. *Beckoning* (Murray Kyle)
7. *Long Way Home* (Nessi Gomes)
8. *A Reminder* (Trevor Hall)
9. *The Grandmother's Song* (Sheffy Oren Bach)

Playlist
SOULutions Songs
on Spotify

SOULvation Meditation: Soaring Home

SOULvation is about being aware of our inherent wholeness. Freed from attachment, triumphing over difficulty, we can see the oneness of everything. We have come home to self with total joyous acceptance and celebration.

(from salvation: liberation from ignorance or suffering, being saved)

SOULvation
reflective intentions

Embrace oneness.

Celebrate that we are free.

Know we are here now.

Inspirations

*The only test of a soul's salvation
is inward happiness.*

LIN YUTANG

*Your true home is not limited by time,
space, nationality or race.*

THICH NHAT HANH

*Nirvana is this moment seen directly.
There is nowhere else than here. The only
gate is now. The only doorway is your own
mind and body. There's nothing else to be.
There's no destination. It's not something
to aim for in the afterlife, it's simply the
quality of this moment.*

BUDDHA

SOULvation Songs Souvenir Playlist – Soaring Home

1. *In Dreams* (Jai-Jagdeesh)
2. *Remember* (Omkara)
3. *Fly High* (Deva Premal & Miten)
4. *Pachamama* (Beautiful Chorus)
5. *Rise Sister Rise Chant* (Rebecca Campbell, Amy Firth)
6. *Blue Sky* (Nick Barber)
7. *This Is The Day* (Jaya Laksmi)
8. *Return to Love* (Susie Ro)
9. *Undying* (Guruganesha Singh)

Playlist
SOULvation Songs
on Spotify

SOULvent Meditation: Rain of Blessings

SOULvent is being grateful for everything we have while not being attached to anything. It's about having enough but not too much. Striving to live sustainably. Living within our means. It's about honouring the planet and not taking too much from Mother Nature. It's about making reparations when we have over-consumed.

(from solvent: able to pay all debts, dissolving, liquifying)

SOULvent
reflective intentions

Accept that we have enough.

Acknowledge that
we are enough.

Live lightly with gratitude.

Inspirations

Detachment is not that you should own
nothing, but that nothing should own you.

ALI IBN ABI TALIB

How much does he lack himself who must
have many things?

SEN NO RIKYU

The philosophy of non-attachment is based
on the understanding that holding on too
tightly to those things, which in any case
are always going to be slipping through our
fingers, hurts, and gives us rope burn.

SURYA DAS

The purpose of human life is to make
best use of the resources that nature or
God has given us.

SWAMI RAMA

SOULvent Songs
Souvenir Playlist –
Rain of Blessings

1. *Rain of Blessings* (Deva Premal & Miten)
2. *Mother I Feel You* (Windsong Martin)
3. *Abundance* (Alexia Chellun)
4. *Blessed We Are* (Peia)
5. *Mahalo* (Mary Isis)
6. *Protect The Water* (Murray Kyle)
7. *Akaal* (Ajeet, Trevor Hall)
8. *Ancient Mother* (Sacred Earth)
9. *New Earth* (Samjjana)

Playlist
SOULvent Songs
on Spotify

Conclusion: Our Mission Possible

We change the world by changing ourselves. By changing what we think, how we feel, what we do and what we believe. This change matters greatly.

Each small act of kindness and compassion adds up. Each individual positive intention builds the whole. Every time we say 'yes' to love, to truth, to peace and to integrity, we are one step closer to the irresistible potential of the Universe.

It's up to us. If not us, who?

The time is now. If not now, when?

The world is waiting for us to wake up, to grow up and to show up.

The invitation is to stop sleep-walking through our lives and to take stock of what we're doing and what we're not doing.

The invitation is to open ourselves to better ways of living, to expand our hearts and our minds, to examine our beliefs and discard those that no longer serve us.

The invitation is to live a more soulful life in harmony with the planet and all sentient beings. To become the ones we've been waiting for. If we don't go within, we'll go without.

This is our opportunity, together. This is our mission possible, should we choose to accept it.

Lokah Samastah Sukhino Bhavantu

Acknowledgements

Acknowledgements – where to start! As I've discovered, it takes a village. So some specific worthy co-conspirators herewith.

First up, thank you to the marvellous Juliette Lachemeier from The Erudite Pen. Juliette and her wonderful team, including cover designer Judith San Nicolas and interior book designer Lorna Hendry, have been such a boon for this neophyte author and have manifested this beautiful version of my thoughts and words. Thanks too to Gloria Webb from Jabiru Publishing who referred me onto Juliette.

A gentle shout out to Nigel Pegrum of Pegasus Recording Studios for the SOUL Meditations Podcast and to Deva Premal for gifting me her Gayathri OM's to top and tail each episode.

An eye-watering accolade goes to Veronica Sagredo from Blue Click Photography for making me look and feel gorgeous.

Harmonious heartfelt gratitude goes to the soulful musicians featured in the nine playlists, with special mention to those I've had the absolute joy of singing with live – Deva Premal & Miten, Sacred Earth, Vanessa Forbes and Kevin James.

A magical thank you goes to Nicole Holzheimer from I Am Therapies for leading me up the Shamanic garden path and helping me open up the portals of creativity.

The Flowing Yogini aka Melisah Feeney deserves a very special soulful acknowledgement as a primary co-conspirator from way back. Melisah has cradled and nurtured my aspirations for many years and is a transformational soul sister. Her beautiful 'Yoga with Soul' YouTube sequences take this book to another level of embodiment. More SOUL adventures to come!

A very special editorial mention also goes out to the esteemed Wendy and Peter Schuetz. Their wise and lovingly strategic very first edit and their ongoing advice lifts me up.

Last but certainly not least I wish to honour my amazing daughter Cloe Jakel and my loving husband Graham Knell. Cloe's skilled and creative mastery has launched me into the digital space to reach further and wider than I'd thought possible. Her insight and practical wisdom give me wings to fly as well as helping me stay grounded when I need it. Graham keeps the home fires burning in our sanctuary with his unconditional love, support and encouragement especially when I'm off somewhere physically or metaphysically!

About the Author

Jill Knell has a professional background in community, organisation, team and personal evolution. She is deeply committed to and specialises in being with people who are focused on co-creating a better world.
Her focus over the last two decades has been the integration of our conscious awareness and spiritual intelligence into our lives and our work.

The author draws her inspiration from the natural world and from a range of eclectic wisdom sources courtesy of the universal library. Jill is naturally optimistic and her disposition is one of light-hearted joy, hope, curiosity and compassion. She learned her first meditation practice when she was fourteen years old. Meditation, in many forms, has been her best friend throughout her life – always there to support her highest purpose and ongoing growth and development.

Jill is attracted to practices that are elegantly simple, graceful, joyful and easily accessible. Her favourite forms of meditation are real-life Soul Strolling (immersed in beauty) and singing mantras and soul songs (ecstatic breath), ideally with others. She is blessed to live in a beautiful sanctuary in tropical Cairns (Australia) with her husband and their canine companion Zinc. They share five children and seven grandchildren. So far.

Enjoyed the book?
You can contact the author at:
Email: jill@soulworking.com
Website: www.soulmaps.com.au

If you liked the book, please leave a
review on Amazon, Goodreads or with
the author directly. Reviews are invaluable
in supporting an author's hard work
and are greatly appreciated.